941.83.

Items sho
showr
borro
teleph
barc
This c
Rene
Fines
incu.
be ch

L

Baile
Dublin

DUBLIN'S FALLEN HERO

HERO

THE LONG LIFE AND SUDDEN DEATH OF NELSON'S PILLAR
1809-1966

by

DENNIS KENNEDY

D1351100

Ormeau Books

BELFAST

First published in 2013 by

Ormeau Books
3 Mornington, Belfast BT7 3JS,
Northern Ireland

© Copyright 2013 Dennis Kennedy
All rights reserved.

ISBN 978-0-9572564-1-5

FOREWORD

Ireland's 'decade of centenaries' (2012-2022) marks a remarkable succession of historic events which convulsed the island of Ireland a century ago and left it divided into two separate and in many ways estranged and at times hostile entities. In the middle of this decade falls not a centenary, but a half-centenary—that of the destruction of Nelson's Pillar in the centre of Dublin in March 1966.

The story of the Pillar, why it was there in the first place, why it survived for so long, and how and why it was destroyed, can help us better understand the misconceptions and conflicting interpretations that surround the events being commemorated, and which continue to block the path to a shared idea of Irishness.

This account of the Pillar, from the first decade of the 19th century to the eve of the latest Northern Troubles in the last third of the 20th century , has its origins in a paper presented to the Belfast Literary Society in 2005 to mark the bi-centenary of the Battle of Trafalgar, and possibly much earlier in my first ascent of the Pillar as a schoolboy in 1946.

Dennis Kennedy
Belfast, 2013.

Note on illustrations

Except where otherwise indicated, illustrations are from the author's own collection of historic prints and postcards. Thanks are particularly due to the National Library of Ireland for permission to reproduce items from its collections, and to the Dublin City Archive, The Cork Historical and Archaeological Journal, the Irish Architectural Archive, the Royal Society of Antiquaries of Ireland, and to Mrs Eithne Clarke and Mr Frank Kelly.

Front cover: O'Connell Street, Dublin, c1950.
Hilda Roberts, HRHA. (1901-1982)

"Remove not the ancient landmark, which thy fathers have set."
Proverbs, Ch. 22 v 28.

1   SOME PUBLIC MONUMENT

Nelson in his glory, Sackville Street c 1820.

Nelson's Pillar, completed in 1809, dominated the centre of Dublin for more than one hundred and fifty years. It was Dublin's Eiffel Tower, its most easily recognised landmark, the hub of the city's tram and bus routes, rendezvous point for its citizens, and the image every visitor wanted to have on the postcard he sent home.

Not everyone liked the 128 foot Doric column with the 10 foot statue of Admiral Lord Nelson on top. Some said it was ugly, far too big for its location in the middle of what was Sackville Street, renamed O'Connell Street in 1924. Others asked why a monument to that most English of heroes was there at all. At various times throughout the 19th century, Dublin City Council, and Irish Members of Parliament at Westminster and, later, Deputies in the

1

Leabharlanna Poibli Chathair Bhaile Átha Cliath
Dublin City Public Libraries

post-independence Dail, called for its removal. But Nelson was still there in 1966, having survived even the destruction all around him during the 1916 Easter Rising.

On the morning of Tuesday March 8th 1966, however, he was eventually, and illegally, blown off his perch. Half the Pillar went with him, and the rest was later demolished. Dublin lost its most distinctive landmark, and the main aspect of the city centre was changed for ever. 'Dublin's Glory' was gone.

ADMIRAL LORD NELSON.

As the Dublin Penny Journal saw him.

Why was Nelson there in the first place? How did it come about that Dublin could confidently claim to be the first city anywhere to honour Lord Nelson with such a public memorial? Completed in August 1809, the Nelson Pillar, to give it its proper title, was among the very earliest great monuments to the hero of Trafalgar. It was to be another 34 years before London created Trafalgar Square with Nelson's Column as its centre-piece.

When the news of the victory at Trafalgar reached Dublin on November 8th, 1805, it was greeted with celebrations in the streets, and *Rule Britannia* was sung in the theatres. The city was illuminated, and at the Mansion House 'an elegant transparency showed Neptune laying his crown at the feet of our gracious sovereign, seated on his throne supported by Britannia and Hibernia'.

The *Freeman's Journal* had 'infinite pleasure' in releasing the news of Nelson's victory to its readers, adding:

Some Public Monument

We congratulate our country upon the glorious defeat of the enemy. To the people of Ireland it should particularly be a matter of great exultation as part of the plan of operations of that fleet which has been so defeated and shattered was an attack on this country.[1]

Ten days later the first move was taken to erect a monument to Nelson. On the 18th of November 1805 the Dublin City Assembly agreed that 'some public monument of respect to that gallant and illustrious hero Lord Viscount Nelson (should) be handed down to posterity'. Less than a week later, on the 23rd, the Lord Mayor of Dublin, Alderman James Vance, called a meeting of the nobility, clergy, bankers, merchants and citizens at the Royal Exchange '...for the purpose of erecting a monument to the memory of Nelson'.

The meeting agreed that a subscription be opened for that purpose 'in order to give to our fellow subjects of every situation an opportunity of contributing to the commemoration of a name equally dear to all ranks'. It also agreed that a committee of Twenty One be appointed '...to whom the entire management and execution of this public object be entrusted'.[2]

On November 27th the city fathers gave further indication of their rejoicing at the victory by going in formal procession — the Lord Mayor, the Recorder, Aldermen, High Sheriffs, Common Council *et al* attended by the City regalia, preceded by a grand band of music — to the Castle and presented to His Excellency the Viceroy, the Earl of Hardwicke, an address of congratulations to His Majesty upon the late glorious victories at sea.[3]

The following day, 28th November, the Nelson committee was set up under the chairmanship of the Lord Mayor, and containing many distinguished names, among them four MPs – John La Touche, Robert Shaw, Hans Hamilton and John Claudius Beresford – as well as two other members of the La Touche family, and one Arthur Guinness.

Reports of that first meeting suggest that John La Touche took the lead in proposing the monument. The La Touches were a French Huguenot family of bankers long settled in Ireland. Coincidentally,

3

the one French admiral who could claim a victory over Nelson was Louis Rene de Latouche-Treville, who had defeated Nelson at Boulogne in 1801. When Latouche, a naval hero to the French of almost Nelsonian standing, died of natural causes later that year, Nelson wrote to a friend that 'Latouche has given me the slip'.

The committee had three main tasks. It had to select the form of the monument and its design, it had to decide where to put it and it had to raise the money to pay for it. Both the form of the monument and its location would affect its cost, so what sort of monument was it to be?

At the time the vogue for the classical was dominating public architecture throughout western Europe, and Greece and Rome provided many examples of how to commemorate a public hero. The best known to architects and men of taste who had travelled was Trajan's column in Rome, a 125 feet high marble pillar on a smallish plinth, with an inner spiral staircase leading to a platform at the top, just beneath the statue. In the event Dublin's Pillar was just slightly taller and looked remarkably similar to Trajan's, without the spiral freeze around the outside which is the distinctive feature of Trajan's column.

Trajan's column, Rome. 19th C print.

While a column was no doubt appropriate to a hero of Nelson's stature, there were not many precedents for it in Irish public architecture. There were some obelisks—at the site of the Battle of the Boyne, erected in 1736, and one on Killiney Hill, 1742. The Phoenix column had been set up in the Park in 1745, but the only pillar with a statue on top was that in Birr in what was then King's County, erected in 1747 to the victor of Culloden, the Duke of Cumberland,

Some Public Monument

That was the brainchild of Sir Laurence Parsons, of Birr Castle, a major landlord in the county. Parsons and some other 'gentlemen of the King's County' raised the Pillar 'at their own expense from a principle of loyalty' and in honour of the Duke for defeating the rebels at Culloden and for defending their civil and religious liberties. Birr Castle itself had been besieged in 1690 during the Williamite Wars by an earlier generation of Jacobite forces.[4]

Early 20th century postcard of the Cumberland Pillar in Birr.

The tall Doric column, by Samuel Chearnley, is still there, though the Duke has been missing for almost a century. Unlike Nelson, the Duke was not illegally blown off his Pillar. Instead he was removed in 1915 by the local authority as a safety measure, the statue having been damaged and in danger of toppling off. One story is that it had been used for target practice by men of a Scottish Highland regiment stationed in Birr, mindful of Culloden where the Duke's crushing of the Scots Jacobites had earned him the nickname 'Butcher Cumberland'.

When, in 1806, the Dublin committee publicised its project it invited the artists of the United Kingdom 'to submit proposals for

5

designs for the intended object', without further specification. It was seemingly left to those wishing to submit a proposal to decide what form the monument would take. The winning entry came from a young English architect, William Wilkins, then aged 29, who proposed a tall Doric column on a plinth, with capital and abacus supporting a Roman Galley. So a column it was.

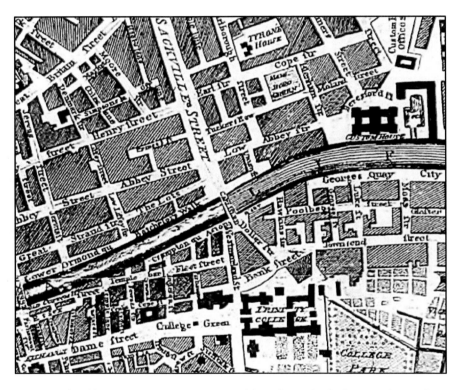

Map of Dublin in 1811, showing location of the Pillar – the dot between the words Sackville and Street. (Courtesy of the National Library of Ireland.)

Just when, or why, it was decided to place it in the middle of Sackville Street is not clear. The street had been, until recently, a broad mall lined by grand houses, most built in the last decades of the 18th century as town residences for the nobility and gentlemen who made up the revivified Irish Parliament, sitting in its superb 18th century building just across the river at College Green. Carlisle

Bridge across the Liffey, linking Sackville Street with Westmoreland Street and the Parliament House, on the south side, had been completed barely a decade earlier, mainly to facilitate access to the Parliament, which, up to that date, had to be approached from the north side via the then lowest river crossing, Essex Bridge.

Though the site of the Pillar later became the acknowledged centre of Dublin, the very heart of the city, this was not yet the case in 1805. But its nearness to the river, and to the dock area, may have made it an appropriate setting for an admiral.

In architectural terms the area was on the way up, and the new Pillar was close to both the former Parliament House and the new Custom House (1791). The migration of the business of the city downstream from the neighbourhood of the Castle was also underway, and the first decade of the 19th century saw many new shops and businesses setting up in Sackville Street.

In some regards, also, the street was on the way down. The abrupt termination of the Irish Parliament meant members of it no longer had any need of fine residences in Dublin, and several houses had already fallen vacant. It was perhaps thought that the erection of a great monument might improve its fortunes.

There was, in a sense, a vacancy for a military hero in Sackville Street. In it there had stood, for some decades, a statue of General Sir William Blakeney, later Lord Blakeney, born in County Limerick in 1671, whose long military career took off during the War of Jenkins' Ear, (1739-48), when he served with distinction at a then little known spot on the south coast of Cuba called Guantanamo Bay.

He was in action again in 1846, this time in Scotland defending Stirling Castle against the Jacobites under Bonnie Prince Charlie, before he and the Castle were relieved by none other than the Duke of Cumberland, shortly before Culloden. During the Seven Years War, Blakeney became something of a national hero for his resolute but unsuccessful defence of the island of Minorca—where he was Lieutenant Governor—against the French in 1757. (Minorca was also to feature frequently in Nelson's Mediterranean service.)

In 1756 the Ancient and Most Benevolent Society of the Friendly Brothers of St Patrick commissioned, and paid for, a statue to General Blakeney by the Flemish sculptor Van Nost. It was unveiled in 1759, on the spot in Sackville Street subsequently occupied by Nelson's Pillar. Blakeney died in 1761 at the age of 90. J.T. Gilbert, in his *History of the City of Dublin*, describes it as a 'pedestrian' statue, presumably as opposed to an equestrian one.[5] It had either fallen into disrepair and had gone by 1805, or was, as one writer says, removed to make way for the Nelson Pillar.[6]

From the start there were divided opinions on the choice of site. A 'very strong protest', according to one source, appeared in leading newspapers, calling for the Pillar to be positioned on the banks of the river, giving the Admiral a view out to sea. [7]

Others suggested a maritime site, such as on Howth Head at the entrance to Dublin Bay. An unattributed drawing (right) in the Irish Architectural Archive dated 1808, believed to be one of the submissions for the monument, shows a large obelisk on a rocky foreshore with a Martello Tower on the cliff behind.[8]

Anonymous design for a monument.
(Courtesy of Irish Architectural Archive.)

One suggestion is that the deciding voice on the choice of Sackville Street was the ultimate authority in Ireland – the Lord Lieutenant, head of the Dublin Castle administration and the monarch's viceroy. Perhaps the fact that that particular spot had been occupied by a public statue may have made it both an obvious choice, and one that presented no great issues of ownership of the parcel of land on which the Pillar was to be built. (This question of ownership was to prove crucial in subsequent debates on whether or not the Pillar should or could be moved.)

The enthusiasm of November 1805 drove forward the movement to commemorate Nelson in Dublin—it was the initiative of the city, not of the Vice-Regal governing machine in Dublin Castle, and not even of the official city, but of the committee of notables set up in November. The local committee decided on the site, and on the winning design, Wilkins' Doric column. It also fell to the committee to raise the money to finance the ambitious project, entirely by public subscription. This third task was to present the committee with much difficulty.

Wilkins' design.
(Courtesy of Irish Architectural Archive)

The estimated cost of Wilkins' proposed Pillar was £5,000, (about £250,000 in today's money) not including the sculpture on top. The Bank of Ireland had paid £40,000 (£320,000) to purchase the Parliament House in College Green a few years earlier.

William Wilkins, (1778-1839) was to become a highly successful architect, best known for his National Gallery in London in what became Trafalgar Square, and for his work on University College London, Downing College and King's College (Cambridge), and many country houses. The Dublin Pillar is generally listed among

9

his early works.

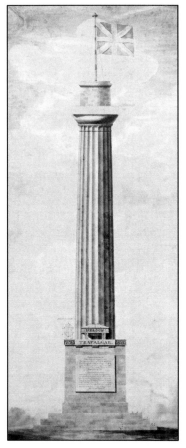

*Johnston's sketch
(Courtesy of the National
Library of Ireland)*

Wilkins' original design had a Roman galley on top, not a statue of Nelson, and at the base a catafalque, with the words 'Nelson' and 'Trafalgar' above and below it.

But Wilkins was not, in the end, commissioned to build the Pillar. The committee 'acknowledged their obligation to William Wilkins Esq, Fellow of Caius College, for that which furnished the groundwork of the beautiful column'. But they went on to say that they could never cease 'to regret that means were not placed in their hands to enable them to gratify him, as well as themselves, by executing his design precisely as he had given it'. They added that 'Francis Johnston Esq. of Dublin, Architect... afforded the necessary assistance.'[9]

Irish writers on the Pillar have tended to highlight Johnston's role in the project, and some ascribe the Pillar to him, pointing to the differences between Wilkins' design and the work as it was finished under Johnston's supervision.

The accounts of the committee, which are detailed, include no record of payment of an architect's fee. Shortage of funds seems to have been the main reason why, having accepted Wilkins' design, the committee felt unable to go ahead with the commission to him.

Francis Johnston, (1760-1829) was eighteen years older than Wilkins and in 1806-7 was already an established architect, having been appointed in 1805 as architect to Dublin's Board of Works and Civil Buildings. He was born in Armagh, the son of an architect, and in 1784 became architect to the Archbishop of Armagh, Primate Robinson. For Robinson he built the Armagh Observatory and was responsible for the interior of what is still today one of the most charming buildings in Northern Ireland – the Archbishop's Chapel in Armagh.

In Dublin he is remembered chiefly for the General Post Office, or the GPO as it is usually known, built almost a decade after the Pillar (1815-1817), the Chapel Royal in Dublin Castle, and for St George's Church in Hardwicke Place—to many the finest church in Dublin. Francis Johnston was also one of the founders of the Royal Hibernian Academy in 1823, and is regarded as the successor to Gandon in the pantheon of Irish architects.

The Pillar as built differed in several ways from Wilkins' original design, most notably in the replacement of the galley on top with a statue of Nelson. The base was also rather different—rugged and foursquare, and larger than Wilkins' more elegant plinth, which was slightly raked in sympathy with the tapering of the column.

These alterations are presumed to be the work of Johnston; a drawing dated 1808 signed by Johnston shows a Pillar similar to Wilkins', with the catafalque and the words Nelson and Trafalgar. It has no statue, but what appears to be a base for one, and also an un-tapered block-like pedestal.

Wilkins' biographer, claims that Wilkins 'had to substitute an indifferent statue of Nelson', as the committee could not afford his original design, and that the committee apologised to him for this in their pamphlet *Nelson's Pillar*, circulated in 1811. In fact the apology, as quoted already, was a general one, with no specific reference to the statue.[10]

The statue was by Thomas Kirk, born in Cork, the son of an Edinburgh father. Kirk was trained in Dublin, and in 1807-8 was still in his twenties. Nelson was one of his first commissions. Opinions on the merits of Kirk's statue of Nelson were to differ as much as they did on the Pillar itself. Maurice Craig found it 'admirable',[11] and it is generally acknowledged that it established Kirk's reputation as a sculptor and helped launch a very successful career.

If cost was the reason why Wilkins' original project could not be carried out, these changes made by Johnston were almost certainly to save money. Whatever the explanation, we can say that Wilkins designed the Pillar, but Johnston was responsible for its erection and, to some extent, for its final appearance.[12]

Wilkins' monument to Nelson at Great Yarmouth. 19thC print

Wilkins used a very similar design for a memorial column to Nelson erected in Great Yarmouth in 1815. His plan as submitted included a ship on top, as in his submission for Dublin, and also had a sarcophagus on one side, as in Dublin. In the event the column was crowned by a statue of Britannia and it is about 10 feet taller than the Dublin work. At Great Yarmouth the column was placed on open ground by the sea – though it has long since been surrounded by industrial buildings. It too had an internal staircase leading to a viewing platform.[13]

Its base resembles the lighter, raked version depicted in Wilkins' Dublin proposal, while the treatment of the statue of Britannia at the top is quite different from that of Nelson in Dublin.

Wilkins later submitted an entry for the commission to design the Wellington Monument in the Phoenix Park, but was unsuccessful. In 1828 he competed for the commission for the statue of the Duke of York in London, submitting drawings of his Dublin and Yarmouth pillars in support, but was again unsuccessful.

The inclusion of a stone spiral staircase within the Dublin Pillar, giving access to the platform at the top just below the statue, was an important feature. The Birr pillar had no inner staircase, nor does London's Trafalgar Square column. In London, Wilkins would have had, close to hand, another Doric column, which has some similarity to the Dublin Pillar, and which had an inner stair—The Monument, designed by Sir Christopher Wren and completed in 1677, to commemorate the Great fire of London of 1666. Its internal staircase, giving access to a viewing platform, to this day attracts some 100,000 visitors yearly, each adult paying £3.00 for the privilege of climbing up, double, in today's money values, the ten pence charged in Dublin in 1809.

The Monument, London.

2   THE FIRST STONE

Laying the first stone, 1808. Contemporary print.
(Reproduced by permission of the Royal Society of Antiquaries of Ireland ©)

The foundation stone for the Pillar was laid, with much pomp and ceremony, on 15th February 1808 by the Lord Lieutenant, the Duke of Richmond, who had succeeded the Duke of Bedford in 1807. Reporting the event, the *Freeman's Journal* said 'there were few who did not experience the throb of nationality when they saw the constituted authorities of their country, and the most respectable citizens of the capital, emulate each other in the demonstration of respect and affection to the memory of a real hero.'

For the ceremony the Duke of Richmond dressed in a General's uniform, accompanied by the Duchess in deep mourning for the dead hero, drove in a state coach drawn by 'six of the most beautiful horses' The procession from Dublin Castle to the site included Horse Yeomanry and Foot Yeomanry, sailors, Officers of the Army and the Navy, subscribers, the committee, the Provost and Fellows of Trinity College, the Lord Mayor, the Common Council, Sheriffs, Aldermen, and Peers according to their degrees.

According to one contemporary report it was considered that the city had 'probably never before seen a grander and more impressive parade'.[14] Another account records that it was a very wet day, that one side of the street was being demolished and was waste ground, with the result that the troops paraded in a sea of mud, and the Rotunda band had 'to sing small' as its drums had lost their tension because of the rain.[15]

The Duke laid the first stone and the yeomanry fired three volleys, followed by a discharge of artillery, the crowd gave three cheers, and the band played 'Rule Britannia'.

The inscription on the brass plate affixed to the foundation stone (left) was in keeping with the grandeur of the occasion.

BY THE
BLESSING OF ALMIGHTY GOD,
TO COMMEMORATE
The transcendant Heroic Achievements of
THE RIGHT HON. LORD VISCOUNT NELSON,
DUKE OF BRONTI, IN SICILY,
Vice-Admiral of the White Squadron of His Majesty's Fleet,
Who fell gloriously in the Battle off
CAPE TRAFALGAR,
On the 21st Day of October, 1805,
WHEN HE OBTAINED FOR HIS COUNTRY
A VICTORY,
OVER THE
COMBINED FLEETS OF FRANCE & SPAIN,
UNPARALLELED IN NAVAL HISTORY.

This first STONE of a Triumphant PILLAR
WAS LAID,
BY HIS GRACE,
CHARLES, DUKE OF RICHMOND AND LENNOX,
Lord Lieutenant General & General Governor of Ireland,
On the 15th Day of February,
IN THE YEAR OF OUR LORD, 1808,
And in the 48th Year of the Reign of our most
GRACIOUS SOVEREIGN,
GEORGE THE THIRD,
In presence of the Committee, appointed by the Subscribers
for erecting this Monument.

For the members of the committee, whose names were appended to the inscription, joy must have been mixed with both relief and anxiety. At a meeting on 31st December 1807 they had noted that to that date they had raised only £3,827, while the estimated cost of the work was now £6,500. This 'manifest inadequacy' they said, had prevented the commencement of the work.

There was some encouragement from the fact that the Duke of Bedford, who had served briefly as Lord Lieutenant in 1806 and 1807, had promised £200, as had his successor the Duke of Richmond. Sir Arthur Wellesley (Chief Secretary from 1807 to 1809 and not yet Duke of Wellington) had put himself down for £108. So the subscription list was reopened, but the response must have been somewhat disappointing for in early February 1808 they were still appealing for subscriptions.

On February 10th the committee published a notice saying that despite all their zeal and diligence to increase the fund to a sum worthy of the nation and of the man, and equal to a highly approved and beautiful plan which had been adopted, they had not attained their object:

> *Under the circumstances they were reduced to the alternatives of either returning the subscriptions already received, or erecting such a monument as the funds would admit of. Having, however, resolved that a monument should be erected, they have ventured on a middle course and adopted a plan which, though the funds will not at present meet, they think a moderate exertion may enable them to accomplish. This plan is simple that it may be inexpensive, without emblem or sculpture.*

The notice went on to say that the Lord Lieutenant had agreed to lay the first stone on the anniversary of Nelson's victory at Cape St Vincent. That being a Sunday, the ceremony took place the following day, February 15th. The notice ended with a further appeal for subscriptions. 'Should the nation...by a general expression, feel that the capital of Ireland should build a prouder Pillar, and that the original and more beautiful design should be adopted, there is still time.'

Despite the shortfall in funding, the committee in January 1808 had agreed a contract with builders, Messrs Thomas Baker and Robert McCartney, to construct the Pillar at an estimated cost of £4,503 on the basis of drawings supplied by Francis Johnston.

The following May the committee were still appealing for help. If they were to complete the objectives announced in February 'there will be wanting a very considerable sum. They trust therefore that the name of Nelson is not yet forgotten, and that those who have omitted to enrol their names will now come forward'. That notice was published regularly in the newspapers throughout the summer.

The final total cost was £6,856.8s 3d, including Thomas Kirk's statue of Nelson. This had added £630 to the bill. Kirk's fee was

The Pillar in 1809. From the Committee's report of 1811. (Courtesy , National Library of Ireland)

£300, while the Portland stone needed cost £243.18s 7d. The Pillar itself was built of black limestone faced with white Wicklow granite, and must have looked very different from the grubby dark Pillar that many may remember.[16]

The list of subscribers makes rather interesting reading. Three Lords Lieutenants each gave £200—the Earl of Hardwick, the Duke of Bedford and the Duke of Richmond—as did David La Touche and Company. Three Chief Secretaries—Sir Arthur Wellesley, Charles Long and William Elliott—gave, respectively, £108.6s.8.d, £100, and £108.6s.8.d. The Earl of Caledon gave £100, the Earl of Castlestewart £50, and George Canning, Foreign, Secretary from 1807 to 1809,

£22.15s.0d. Dublin Corporation gave £200, Trinity College £100, and the three Guinnesses—Arthur, Benjamin and William—together managed £25.

Various military units made contributions, among them the Officers and Privates of the Sandymount Yeomanry who chipped in four pounds seven shillings and sixpence, and the Crews of the Dublin Gun Boats who donated one day's pay worth £7.11.10. A day's pay from the Newtown-Mount-Kennedy Cavalry added £5.1s.4d and Two 'Old Sea Officers' gave £5.13.9 each, as did one aptly named Horatio Nelson Vigors.

In all a total of more than 230 separate donations was recorded by the committee, from individuals, clubs, businesses and serving military. The largest single donation came from the Patriotic Fund (£341.5.0) while the remainder varied from £200 down to £1. In the end the committee found itself in pocket. The total income, from the subscriptions and other receipts came to £7,138.7.2, leaving a balance of £281.18.11. Oddly missing from the list of subscribers is Lord Castlereagh – surely the most prominent Irish aristocrat politician of the time.

He had been Chief Secretary in Ireland from 1798 to 1801, responsible for piloting the Act of Union through the Irish Parliament. More relevant, he was Secretary of State for War in London in 1805, which made him Nelson's political boss at the time of Trafalgar. It was Castlereagh in person who gave Nelson his sailing orders in London before the Trafalgar campaign.

Castlereagh was once more Secretary of State for War when the Pillar committee appealed for subscriptions in 1807. Also missing from the list is Castlereagh's father, Lord Londonderry of Mount Stewart in County Down.

It was Castlereagh who first formally proposed, in the House of Commons on January 28th, 1806, that a suitable monument be erected to Nelson in St. Paul's Cathedral in London.[17] It was not completed until 1818, and it was 1843 before the Admiral finally took his place on top of his great memorial column in Trafalgar Square.

3   WHY DUBLIN?

NELSON'S PILLAR

One of the earliest depictions of the Pillar, c 1811.
(Courtesy of the National Library of Ireland.)

By the second half of 1809 the Pillar was complete. It was opened to the public on Trafalgar Day, the 21st of October, the fourth anniversary of the battle. The citizens of Dublin were offered an

19

unprecedented perspective on their city. For the payment of ten pence, they could climb the 168 steps to the viewing platform. For the next 157 years its ascent was a must on every visitor's list.

It was a monument to a great English hero and to his defeat of the French at Trafalgar, built in the heart of the capital of a country which had, over the previous decade, seen two rebellions against English rule, both of which had sought the support of the French enemy, and one of which had seen a French force invading Ireland and, initially, routing a British army.

It was a monument built and largely paid for by citizens of Dublin. The initiative for it came from the city, neither from London nor from Dublin Castle, the seat of British administration in Ireland. But it was the Dublin of the Ascendancy, Protestant Dublin — Anglican, not Presbyterian. Some of the growing Catholic population, including merchants and professionals, may have cheered the ceremonial laying of the first stone, and rejoiced in Nelson's victory, but they had no representation in the city Corporation. The long list of individual subscribers to the cost of the Pillar does not appear to include anyone identifiably Catholic.

At its final meeting in June 1811 the committee handed the Pillar over to four Trustees — John Leland Maquay, Peter Digges La Touche, Randall McDonnell and Arthur Guinness. And it was all paid for — some 230 subscribers, plus income on money deposited, had raised a total of more than £7,000. The surplus of £281.18s 11d, was invested in government stocks to help pay for the Pillar's upkeep. It was agreed that an admission fee would be extracted from those who wanted a closer look at Nelson and an unparalleled view of the city and this too would help pay the cost of upkeep[18].

Despite the delays, the completion of the monument within four years of Trafalgar was a remarkable achievement, and put Dublin among the first major cities anywhere in the world so to honour Nelson. Strictly speaking it was not the first, for Glasgow had built its large memorial obelisk — no statue — to Nelson on Glasgow Green in 1806. Montreal produced a column and statue similar to Dublin's on the banks of the St Lawrence by 1809, at almost exactly the same time as the completion of Nelson's Pillar.[19]. Birmingham managed a grandiose statue by October 1809. Edinburgh's memorial—the signal tower on Carleton Hill—was started in 1807 but not completed until 1816.

Nelson's Column, Trafalgar Square, London

The city of London, strange to say, had no monument in an open public space to the great hero until 1843, when Nelson took his place on top of his column in the newly created Trafalgar Square.

The whole project took three more decades to finish, and the four great lions – part of the original design—were not put in place until 1867.

Initially the column was, like the Dublin Pillar, in the hands of a Nelson Memorial committee, and was to be financed through public subscription. But, even more than in Dublin, there was difficulty raising the amount needed. In 1844 the Government took over financing and completion of the column. Objections to its proposed height, on the grounds that it was out of proportion to the new National Gallery, meant it was reduced by 30 feet after work on the site had commenced. (Nelson still stood some 38 feet taller in London than he did in Dublin – the total height of the column is 172 feet, the Pillar was 134.)

Why Dublin's rush to commemorate Nelson? The Admiral had no particular personal connection with Dublin, or indeed with Ireland, though one of his several lady loves did settle here.[20] He almost certainly never visited Dublin, and it was not a naval base. It would seem Nelson was not much enamoured of Irish national aspirations. Serving in the Caribbean in 1785 he reportedly refused an invitation to a St Patrick's Day function on the island of St Kitts because the town was flying 'Irish flags' hoisted by, in Nelson's words, 'vagabonds'.[21]

When Nelson died at Trafalgar in 1805, Ireland was part of the recently created United Kingdom of Great Britain and Ireland, and Dublin had fair claim to be the second city of that kingdom. In size, only London surpassed it. The previous fifty years had seen the city transformed and beautified—new streets and squares surrounded by fine Georgian terraces had been created, and great public and private buildings erected.

The Parliament House dated back to 1729 and was followed by a succession of neo-classical Georgian masterpieces—Leinster House (1745), the west front of Trinity College (1752), the Rotunda (1751), Charlemont House (1762), the Royal Exchange, now the City Hall (1762), the Four Courts (1786) and the splendid new Custom House (1791). By the end of the century Dublin looked very much a capital city.

The Act of Union of 1800, however, robbed it of its Parliament and lessened its status as a capital. The United Irishmen's rebellion of 1798 and its suppression had spread unrest throughout the island, including Dublin. While the work of enhancing the city did not come to an abrupt halt—the Post Office was still to come, and the Chapel Royal and the King's Inns were still being built when the Pillar went up—Dublin's era of Georgian magnificence was coming to an end.

Why Dublin?

That era, however, had produced comparatively little by way of monuments and statues. William III had been on his horse in College Green since 1701, joined by George I in the Mansion House Gardens (1743) and by a very imposing George II on horseback in St Stephen's Green (1756). And General Blakeney had come and gone from Sackville Street.

Nelson's Pillar was a different category of public monument — truly imperial in concept and size, and given unrivalled prominence in its location, it could claim to be the triumphant culmination of the most remarkable period in the architectural history of Dublin, even if not everyone hailed its beauty.

The Post Office with base of Pillar to right.   Geo Petrie, c1830.

The driving force behind this extraordinary creativity had been the elite of Dublin, variously called the New English, the Ascendancy, or the Anglo-Irish. Some were aristocrats, others were members of the rising prosperous merchant class, or of the professions. All were Protestant. Catholics at that time would have been in a substantial majority in the city, but they had no voice in its governance. The

Protestant elite controlled the various nominating bodies who decided who would sit on the all-Protestant city council.

They would almost certainly have regarded themselves as English, but they were, like the most renowned among them, Jonathon Swift (1667-1745), a special class of Englishmen — Englishmen born in Ireland.

Like Swift many of them would also have been termed 'patriots', particularly after 1782 when the Irish Parliament (all Protestant) became known as the Patriot Parliament, using its enhanced degree of independence from Westminster to champion Irish interests, meaning essentially the interests of the English in Ireland as opposed to the interests of England itself.

This was the patriotism of a small minority, probably no more than 10% in a predominantly Catholic island. In the 1790s a different patriotism manifested itself in the Society of United Irishmen, Protestant led — mostly Presbyterian — but relying on mainly Catholic support outside the province of Ulster. It was different too in that it demanded not enhanced powers for the Dublin Parliament, or the remedying of particular grievances, but total separation from England, and in its seeking, and eventually receiving support for an armed uprising from England's mortal enemy, France.

The insurrection of June 1798, supported by the landing of a French force in the west of Ireland, was a serious and bloody rebellion — brutally suppressed — but it did not attract the popular supports its leaders had called for and the French had expected, and both the rising and the invasion were soon defeated. It had, however, alerted London to the danger posed by Ireland in the context of the war with revolutionary France that had been engulfing most of Europe since 1792.

The Act of Union was, in part, a security measure under which it was hoped a more firmly and fairly governed Ireland would no longer be a source of weakness. (It was widely believed that the Union would soon lead to Catholic Emancipation and the removal of the last restrictions on the Catholic majority, particularly the ban on Catholics entering Parliament. As a result numbers of better-off Catholics supported the Union, as did some prominent Catholic churchmen.)

Emancipation was not achieved until 1829, by which time Catholic discontent had been channelled into organised political action, which soon found a new objective in Home Rule and the end of the Union.

When the Pillar was built in 1808-09, some among the growing Catholic population in Dublin may have regarded Nelson as no hero of theirs, but many more, of all classes and creeds, would have had strong family and personal reasons to rejoice at the victory of Trafalgar. It is estimated that one quarter to one third of the sailors who manned Nelson's fleet were from Ireland, including 400 from Dublin.[22]

Britain's National Archive's listing of all Royal Navy personnel who fought at Trafalgar includes fifty-nine Murphys, all but two with Irish home addresses, and the same number of Sullivans, all but three with Irish addresses.

Some Irish-born officers played prominent roles in the battle. The captain of the *Tonnant*, was Dublin-born Captain Charles Tyler, and of the 500 men serving under him 128 were Irish. The ship's casualties that day included 22 killed. Captain Tyler was among those wounded.

The commander of the marines aboard Nelson's flagship, *Victory*, was Captain Charles William Adair, from County Antrim, of the prominent Ballymena family. He fought on deck alongside Nelson in repelling the attempt by the *Redoubtable* to board the *Victory*, was wounded and then took a second hit and died.

Captain Henry Blackwood, who commanded the frigate *Euryalus*, was on the *Victory* with Nelson as the battle commenced. He was the son of Sir John Blackwood of Ballyleidy (now Clandeboye), County Down, and Dorcas, Baroness Dufferin. A close colleague of Nelson, he witnessed the disputed codicil to Nelson's will just before the battle. Having failed to persuade Nelson, for his own safety, to direct the battle from his frigate rather than from the *Victory*, Blackwood was sent back to his own ship. He survived Trafalgar and ended up Vice-Admiral Sir Henry Blackwood.

Dr William Beatty, the surgeon who tended the dying Nelson on the *Victory*, though often described as Scottish, was born in Londonderry.[23]

Martello Tower at Sandymount

All Dubliners in 1805 would still have had the French invasion of 1798 — and the failed expeditions to Bantry Bay and Lough Swilly — fresh in their memories. In 1803 Emmet's rebellion had again raised the spectre of French invasion. Emmet had been part of the United Irish delegation which had travelled to France to seek support for a rising in Ireland, and he had met Napoleon – then First Consul — and discussed with him French aid for an Irish rebellion.[24] Napoleon had displayed considerable interest in another French expedition to Ireland, and in January 1805 had ordered his fleet at Brest to prepare to land troops in Ireland. This order was intercepted by the British secret service, and while historians now believe it was part of a grand Napoleonic bluff, it was enough to alarm both government and public in Britain and Ireland.

Dubliners would have had at hand immediate and physical evidence of the French threat in the extensive building programme of Martello Towers around the city, which had begun in 1804 to meet the dangers of attack by sea. About 50 of these towers were built in the vicinity of Dublin, and would have been highly visible – as some still are today—and daily reminders of the French danger.

It would be rash to assume that even the most politically aware Catholics, particularly those among the rising middle and professional classes in Dublin would have regarded Nelson as other than a hero, or would have been incensed at the idea of raising a great monument to him.

Daniel O'Connell, for instance, was no radical separatist or admirer of revolutionary France. While studying law in Dublin in 1797 he had been so alarmed at the threat of a French invasion in support of a United Irish rebellion that he sought the permission of his uncle (and patron) to join the Yeomanry, and did, it seems, enlist in the Lawyers Yeomanry Corps.

In 1803 he was explicit in his condemnation of the armed rebellion led by Robert Emmet in July of that year. Writing to his wife in August he said:

> *Young Emmett (sic) is, they say, arrested in Dublin and if he has been concerned in the late insurrection, of which I fear there is no doubt, he merits and will suffer the severest punishment. For my part I think pity would be almost thrown away at the contriver of the affair of 23rd July. A man who could so coolly prepare so much bloodshed, so many murders – and such horrors of every kind, has ceased to be an object of compassion.[25]*

The elite Protestant merchants and bankers who combined to build the Pillar would have shared those sentiments, but would have had other reasons too, commercial and political, to celebrate the victor and his victory. The French blockade had cost the Dublin merchants dear and the significance of Nelson's victory in restoring freedom of the high seas would have been apparent to them.

They would also have been aware of the wider significance of Nelson's victories, culminating at Trafalgar, in the epic struggle with France. Britain and Ireland had been engaged in a war with revolutionary France which was different in kind from anything that had preceded it in Europe. This conflict was not about rival states adjusting the balance of power or squabbling over territory, it was about the survival or destruction of states, about the overthrow of regimes, order and religion as these had been understood.

Nelson's victory was a turning point in this struggle. As one of his biographers has put it, his heroic role was played out in the context of a total British response to the revolutionary era that generated a new national identity, of which Nelson himself became the central figure. Around him coalesced the very concept of Britain, '...a state committed to God, King, parliament and liberty'.[26]

Nelson was a popular hero before his death at Trafalgar. After the Battle of Cape St Vincent in 1797, when Jervis was in command and Nelson his subordinate, it was Nelson who returned to a hero's welcome, a knighthood, the freedom of the city of London and promotion to Rear Admiral Sir Horatio. After the Battle of the Nile in 1798 he became Baron Nelson, and his popularity soared even higher after Copenhagen in 1801, when he became Viscount Nelson. He was portrayed, on prints and paperweights (above) as the saviour of the nation, often with religious overtones, the icon of a newly emerging Britishness, shared by many, but by no means all in Ireland.

One Irishman may have been so impressed by Nelson's victories that he changed his name in his honour. In 1802, when Patrick Brunty, or Prunty, of County Down, registered as a student at St John 's College Cambridge he did so as Patrick Brontë. According to some accounts, the father of Charlotte, Anne and

Why Dublin?

Emily changed his name as a mark of respect for the Duke of Bronté, which title the King of Naples had bestowed on Nelson in 1799. Patrick's son Branwell Bronté wrote a poem in honour of Nelson.

The Dublin establishment would have been anxious to emphasise its loyalty to the new United Kingdom, and Dublin's importance as the second city of the kingdom. It would also have been eager to assert its Britishness, and the Britishness of Ireland, and what more appropriate way of doing this could there be than erecting a great monument to the man who had heroically embodied that Britishness.

Nelson in Montreal. 19th C print

Similar ideas may have moved some of the backers of the Montreal monument. Captured by the British from the French in 1760, Montreal was still a largely French settlement with no more than 8,000 inhabitants. But it had acquired a strong merchant elite of Scottish fur traders, who had fled Scotland after the 1745 Jacobite rebellion.

By 1805 the families of these Scots were beginning to dominate the commercial life of Montreal, and were anxious to assert their Britishness and their recently acquired loyalty.

Nelsons' victory was also welcomed by French residents of the city, who were no friends of revolutionary France and no admirers of Napoleon. The fact that Nelson had spent a month in Quebec in the early days of his naval service—long enough to fall passionately in love with a local teenager— provided a personal link

The Montreal column, restored some years ago, has survived efforts by Quebec nationalists to have it removed.

Neither the Act of Union, nor Nelson's achievement in thwarting Napoleon's war aims, brought stability to Ireland. The agitation of the 1790s and the rebellions of 1798 and 1803, left Ireland at the time of Trafalgar in a state of considerable unrest. The failure to enact Catholic Emancipation greatly stimulated organised political activity among the dominant majority Catholic population. First focused on emancipation, after 1829 this turned to the demand for Home Rule, meaning the end of the Union and the restoration of the Parliament in Dublin.

Even Protestant Dublin was less than resolutely Unionist; the city merchants soon claimed that the loss of the Irish Parliament had damaged their interests. By 1810 they were sufficiently disillusioned with the Union for the City Assembly to pass a resolution calling for the restoration of the Irish Parliament, and for them to invite the rising leader of the Catholic movement, Daniel O'Connell, to address what was termed an 'aggregate meeting', to which Catholic Freemen of the City were invited as well as Protestant.[27]

If the Pillar had not been built when it was, it would probably never have been built at all. By 1830 popular demand was focused on the repeal of the Union and erecting a monument to Nelson would have been strongly resisted. Certainly after the Municipal Reform Act of 1840, when O'Connellites were able to win a majority on Dublin Corporation, and their leader became Lord Mayor, it would have been impossible.

The building of the massive monument to Nelson may have been the Ascendancy's last hurrah.

As the 19th century progressed and Dublin's population grew rapidly, so did the demand for Irish self-government; some began to see Nelson on his Pillar as symbolic of English/British domination. But as the politicians grumbled about Nelson, and repeatedly launched schemes to have him moved, or removed, and replaced on the top of the Pillar by someone more congenial, Nelson and his Pillar became more and more not just part of Dublin, but the very centre of Dublin.

Dublin, and Nelson, welcome King George IV, August 17, 1821, and (below) Daniel O'Connell in triumphal procession after his release from prison in 1844. (Prints, courtesy National Library of Ireland.)

In the years after the building of the Pillar, Sackville Street rapidly gained in importance as the city's centre of gravity moved downstream along the line of the Liffey, towards the commercial activity of the port. An indication of this was the decision to place the new General Post Office, commenced in 1814, right beside the Pillar, at the corner of Sackville Street and Henry Street.

By the mid-19th century the street was the undisputed heart of the city—its principal social boulevard and shopping street, a meeting place, a venue for celebrations and displays. In 1864 it was the obvious place to erect a memorial to Ireland's own great national hero, the Liberator, Daniel O'Connell. (It was another two decades before the grandiose monument was completed.) When the time came, at the end of the century, to honour another national hero, Charles Stewart Parnell, the chosen site had to be the other end of O'Connell Street. From the early 20th century they shared the street with Nelson towering over them.

The Post Office illuminated by electric light from Nelson's Pillar for the visit to Dublin of Queen Victoria and Prince Albert in 1853. (Illustrated London News)

The Trustees of the Pillar continued to mark the anniversaries of Nelson's four great victories by flying the Union flag from the Pillar annually on Trafalgar Day, 21st October, and on the dates of the battles of Cape St. Vincent, Copenhagen and The Nile. In 1905 the centenary of Trafalgar saw the Pillar dressed overall in flags and streamers.

4 A NEAT AND HANDSOME PILLAR

New neighbours: Nelson and the GPO, 1830. Geo.Petrie RHA.

At the time of its construction, opposition to and criticism of the monument was almost entirely non-political—rather it was related to the location of the Pillar and its effect on traffic, and to its aesthetic qualities, not to the merits, political or moral, of the man on top. The one adverse political comment cited by historians

33

appeared in the *Irish Magazine* of September 1809 on the occasion of the placing of Nelson's statue on top of the Pillar. It said the event excited no notice and was marked with indifference on the part of the Irish public, who had little interest in the triumphs of a Nelson or a Wellesley.

The writer commented that these might extend English dominion and trade, and perpetuate English glory, but '...an Irish mind had no substantial reasons for thinking ...that our prosperity or our independence will be more attended to'. The piece ended on a note of high rhetoric:

> *We have changed our gentry for soldiers, and our independence has been wrested from us, not by the arms of France, but by the gold of England. The statue of Nelson records the glory of a mistress and the transformation of our senate into a discount office.*

That final scornful comment referred to the Bank of Ireland's purchase of the old Parliament building in College Green. The *Irish Magazine* was the publication of Watty Cox, a one-time supporter of the United Irishmen, an eccentric and a scourge of Dublin Castle.

Generally the Pillar was welcomed, both as an adornment to the city, and as an appropriate memorial to a great hero. A book published in 1811 entitled *The Picture of Dublin for 1811*, carried a fine engraving which must be among the earliest representations of the new monument, and described it as:

> *..a neat and handsome Pillar, on top of which is a gallery and a statue of Lord Nelson, leaning against a capstan of a ship, well executed. It is surrounded with iron palisades and lamps . From the top an excellent view of the city and bay may be obtained. It is now open to the public; the price of admittance is ten pence.*

But there were some who did not like it, or at least did not like it where it was. One of the most savage criticisms of it came in the 1818 *History of Dublin* by Warburton, Whitelaw and Walsh:

> *It is of most ponderous proportion which is not relieved by the least decoration. Its vastly unsightly pedestal is nothing better than a*

quarry of cut stone, and the clumsy shaft is divested of either base or what can properly be called a capital. Yet with all this baldness and deformity it might have had a good effect when viewed at a distance, or placed somewhere else; but it not only obtrudes its blemishes on every passenger, but actually spoils and blocks up our finest street, and literally darkens the other two streets opposite, which though spacious enough, look like lanes.

The writers go on to comment that the original objections to its site had now become '... still stronger since the building of the new Post Office near to it, for by contrast it in great measure destroys the effect of one of the largest and finest porticos in Europe.'

One must presume that Francis Johnston, architect of the GPO and overseer of the building of the Pillar, did not share this view. Messrs W, W and W were harsh critics; in the same book they described the Wellington monument—not then built, but approved and exhibited as a model—as an absurdity and a deformity, heavy, bald and frigid.

But others liked the Pillar, and many commented on how it enhanced the street, helping fill the broad empty space stretching from the river to Rutland Square (now Parnell Square.) In the years since, opinions have been divided on its architectural merits. W. B. Yeats said it was not a beautiful object, and that it divided the street, spoiling the vista. Maurice Craig, the architectural historian, on the other hand, writing in 1952, thought it both beautiful and well-placed, 'Dublin's most conspicuous and most discussed monument', and for good measure he added that, with the Post Office it helped to redeem O'Connell Street, potentially so beautiful, from a squalid disorder almost equal to parts of London.'[28]

Prince Hermann Ludwig Heinrich von Puckler-Muskau, who visited Dublin in 1828, found the Pillar to be 'without taste', as indeed he found the statue of William the Third at College Green. He did not like the Castle, with its 'miserable state apartments', or the monument at Kingstown harbour to mark the visit of George IV, while the Wellington obelisk was 'ill-proportioned'.

Thackeray was more easily pleased, and admired the broad and handsome Sackville Street with Nelson on his Pillar. 'In front of Carlisle Bridge,' he wrote 'and not in the least crowded though in the midst of Sackville Street, stands Nelson upon a stone Pillar. The Post Office is on his right hand (only it is cut off).'

Sackville St. c1840, from drawing by W.H.Bartlett.

Thackeray's viewpoint clearly gave him a decent perspective on the Pillar, but close up the view of it was dominated by the large and rather brutal blockhouse on which it stood. The heavy base also blocked off the view from either Henry Street or North Earl Street. *The Dictionary of Dublin, a Complete Illustrated Guide to Dublin*, published in 1908, exactly a century after work had begun on the Pillar, declared it to be 'exceedingly ugly' and 'awkwardly situated'. Old postcards show just how massive the Pillar's base was in relation to passing tramcars, to the street in general and to the GPO in particular.

Many prints based on earlier drawings, however, tend to display some artistic license in exaggerating the width of the street and generally enhancing the Pillar's setting. Bartlett's depiction of Sackville Street in about 1840 goes further and achieves what opponents of the Pillar never managed— he seems to have moved it the full length of the façade of the GPO, forward towards the river.

In the course of the 19th century, while the city changed dramatically, the monument remained largely unchanged. Some minor alterations were made early on; the ornamental railings around the base, seen in early prints, disappeared, as did the catafalque on the side over the name Nelson. Thus exposed, the steps at the base became a favourite resting place for what Thackeray called 'loungers'.

The one major alteration was made in 1894, when the original sub ground level entrance was replaced by one at street level, and a new heavy porch was added with the name Nelson over it, adding to the formidable impact of the base. The railings were reinstated. By that date the original ten pence admission charge had been reduced to three pence.

From the start the opponents of the siting of the Pillar had argued that it would obstruct traffic. The concern was not the effect on traffic along Sackville Street, but on the then much busier route from west to east, that is along Henry Street from the heart of the city and down North Earl Street and Cope Street (later re-named Talbot Street) towards the Custom House and the docks. The Pillar was slap in the middle of the intersection of this route with Sackville Street. As the century progressed, the traffic became heavier and demands that the Pillar be moved, or removed, began to be heard. A plan for the future development of Dublin exhibited at the exhibition of 1853 proposed this, and there were suggestions that it be relocated to one of the city's squares.

This was discussed by the Corporation in 1876, but came to nothing because of the legal status of the Pillar. It was vested in the trustees and would require an act of Parliament to move it; the Corporation had no powers to touch it. Six years later, in 1882, legislation at Westminster—the Moore St Market and North Dublin City Improvement Act—actually authorised the dismantling of the

Pillar and its re-erection further along Sackville Street, towards the northern end, close to where Parnell now stands.

This was to be done by the Moore Street Market Company, set up under the Act, within a strict timetable laid down in the Act, which meant its re-erection had to begin within one month of its dismantling, and had to be completed within two years, on pain of a hefty recurring fine. Once done to the satisfaction of the Board of Works Engineer and of the Trustees, the company would take over all responsibility for the Pillar. It never happened, partly because it would have cost too much, certainly much more than the funds held by the Trustees. So the authority to move the Pillar lapsed, and it stayed where it was.

There was, at the time, vehement opposition to the proposal to move the Pillar; *The Irish Builder*, in July 1882, deemed it a 'ridiculous scheme' and welcomed its failure. Without Nelson's Pillar, it stated, Sackville Street would be robbed of its fair proportions; to remove it would be 'to deprive us of the proud boast of possessing the finest street in Europe'. To say that the Pillar was 'in the way' was absurd.[29]

The motivation behind the campaign to move the Pillar seems to have been non-political and directly related to traffic problems. The sponsors of the Bill included prominent Protestant firms such as Findlaters, and indeed Arthur Guinness—the then head of which firm had sat on the original committee in 1805, and was one of the first Trustees. Their common interest was as owners and operators of drays hauling heavy loads across Dublin. The fact that the Pillar formed a massive block to traffic trying to cross from Henry Street into North Earl Street and vice versa was the nub of the problem.

Less than a decade later the Pillar was again before the Westminster Parliament, this time in the form of a Private Bill of 1891 promoted by prominent tradesmen in Sackville Street, and entitled simply the Nelson's Pillar (Dublin) Bill. Once again traffic was cited as the reason for moving the Pillar, and once again it was envisaged that it would be dismantled and re-erected. Some political flavour was given to the debate on the Second Reading in the Commons by the fact that all opposition to it came from northern Unionists. (Political objections to Nelson had become more frequently heard after Dublin Corporation came under Nationalist control in the 1840s.) But the argument was still largely framed in non-political terms.

Opposing the second reading Mr McCartney, the MP for Antrim South, said the proponents of the Bill had to prove three things:

- That the Pillar was a serious obstacle to traffic
- That its removal would benefit traffic
- And that the proposal to move it had the general assent of the citizens of Dublin.

It seems its supporters were able to convince the House on those matters, for the Bill passed its second reading, but before it could go to committee it was withdrawn, partly because several petitions against it had come from Dublin interests, partly because the Trustees had declared themselves against it, and probably also because of the unresolved question of who was going to pay for the work.

Still, agitation continued for at least the relocation of the Pillar away from its position in the middle of Sackville Street. In July 1890 *The Irish Builder* reported that signatures were being collected for a petition, coming from the residents of the surrounding streets and 'of Dublin and suburbs generally' against moving it.

The drafters of the petition declared that the Nelson Monument '...is now and has been for many years an ancient and useful landmark', that they were satisfied, from their many years' experience, that it caused no obstruction to city traffic, and that the proposed change of site would confer no substantial benefit on the public generally, and could divert traffic, and business from the neighbourhood of its present location. The petition concluded with an appeal to the Irish Members of Parliament and 'the authorities' not to support this proposed change.[30]

So the Pillar stayed where it was. It was part of Dublin, and the life of Dubliners. Its centrality to the city, both physical and social, is nowhere more graphically illustrated than in the most celebrated book on Dublin—James Joyce's *Ulysses.* Joyce's account of his characters' wanderings around the city in June 1904 is meticulous in its detailing of the city's streets and buildings. Joyce himself claimed that his picture of Dublin in *Ulysses* was '...so complete that if the city one day suddenly disappeared from the earth it could be reconstructed out of my book'.

That picture had Nelson's Pillar at its very centre, or as the heading above the main passage referring to the Pillar has it—"In the heart of the Hibernian Metropolis'.

O'Connell Bridge, and Sackville Street, Dublin

This card, posted in May 1905, shows Dublin as it was less than a year after Joyce's 'Bloomsday'.

In *Ulysses*, Joyce lists the destinations of the trams which '...before Nelson's Pillar slowed, shunted, changed trolley' and started out for their various suburbs, and in so doing gives an image of the whole city as a network of tramway lines all converging at the Pillar.[31]

Some pages later Joyce has two ordinary Dublin women deciding they want to do what generations of both Dubliners and visitors wanted to do—go up the Pillar and see the views of Dublin from the top. Again the image of Dublin as a web with Nelson at the centre emerges as the two start to identify the domes of the various churches around the city.

There are other references to Nelson and his Pillar, generally irreverent, as in 'Horatio (one-handled) Nelson', or the 'onehandled adulterer'. Eventually, in the later stages of the book, Bloom himself climbs the Pillar, if not in reality then in hallucination. After passing through several walls he 'climbs Nelson's Pillar, hangs from the top ledge by his eyelids, eats twelve dozens oysters (shells included), heals several sufferers from King's evil' and performs several other fantastical feats.[32]

Nelson even finds his way into Joyce's *Finnegans Wake* with at least two decipherable mentions—one to 'the pillary of the Nilsens' and another to Nelson and his 'trifulguryous pillar'. A generation later, Louis MacNeice, in his 1939 poem *Dublin*, has 'Nelson on his Pillar, watching his world collapse'.

In time, Dubliners took the Pillar to their hearts. A familiar and very large if rather scruffy piece of the city's furniture, it was *The* Pillar, Dublin's Pillar, rather than Nelson's Pillar. Nor was it just, or even primarily, a monument—it was also an outing, an experience. Anyone paying his money could go up the inner staircase and see Dublin from a unique vantage point. When it was built, and for most of its lifetime, the thrill of climbing the Pillar and looking down on the city from a height of 100 feet was, for all but steeplejacks and hot-air balloonists, something totally new.

Over the years both Nelson and the Pillar lent their names to neighbouring features of the Dublin landscape; there was, and still is, a Nelson Street, there was a Nelson Lane, a Nelson Place and a Nelson Café. The café eventually expanded into The Pillar Café Restaurant and Tea Rooms, and had for company a Pillar Picture House, and a Pillar Pharmacy.

THE NELSON PILLAR, O'CONNELL STREET, DUBLIN.

Early postcard showing trams dwarfed by the Pillar's base

The Pillar survived the widespread destruction during the Easter
Rising in 1916, and during the Civil War in 1922-23, conflicts which
saw some of Dublin's architectural masterpieces such as the Four
Courts and the Custom House seriously damaged.   One of the
many ironies surrounding Nelson and his Dublin perch is that his

monument in Great Yarmouth—designed by Wilkins and similar to the Dublin Pillar apart from having Britannia instead of a Nelson on top—was in almost as much danger of demolition in Easter Week as was the Dublin Pillar. On the night of April 24/25, 1916, that is Easter Monday to Tuesday, Great Yarmouth was bombarded by the German High Sea Fleet.

Yarmouth was a naval base and an important target for the Germans, as was Lowestoft which was also shelled. Other east coast towns were targeted by Zeppelins in a prelude to the great naval Battle of Jutland. The timing of the raids was also possibly meant to coincide with the Easter Rising, of which the Germans had prior warning.

Postcard of the destruction in Sackville Street after Easter Week 1916..

Photographs of Sackville Street after the Easter Rising show the Pillar unscathed between the ruined shell of the GPO on one side, and the wreckage of the Imperial Hotel and Clerys on the other.

At one point in Easter week, consideration was given to demolishing it with artillery fire. On Tuesday morning Patrick Pearse, the leader of the rebels, had ordered the occupation of the buildings on the other side of the street from the GPO as a means of strengthening his garrison's position. Communication across the street was greatly aided by the Pillar, which provided cover from fire along the street for those making the dash to and fro.

A senior British officer asked the artillery battery at Trinity College if they could demolish the Pillar with shell-fire. He was told they could, but only the column itself, not the base which was providing the cover, and that demolishing the column would simply fill the street with rubble and provide even more cover. So he decided against it.[33]

After independence in 1921 many thought it ironic, to say the least, that the great British hero should continue to hold pride of place in Ireland's capital city, and that he should do so in close proximity to the GPO—a shrine for Irish Republicanism and Irish nationalism generally following its central role in the 1916 Rising.

So it was inevitable that there would be renewed demands on political grounds for the removal of Nelson. But objections to the Pillar as an obstacle to traffic and on aesthetic grounds also continued.

In 1923 the Dublin Citizens Association voted for its removal. The Association, set up in 1908, had the backing of many of Dublin's major commercial concerns, and ratepayers, and was an energetic watchdog over city matters. In 1925 the Dublin Civic Survey said the site was quite unsuitable, and there should be legislation to permit the Pillar's removal. The Dublin Metropolitan Police Association also wanted it moved. In 1926 the Citizens Association again called on the Corporation to move the Pillar.

The changed political climate seems to have influenced views on aesthetics and town planning. In 1882, as we have seen, *The Irish Builder*, was among the Pillar's stoutest defenders, deeming a plan to remove it 'ridiculous', and warning that that would destroy the proportions of 'the finest street in Europe'. In 1923 when the journal, now called *The Irish Builder and Engineer*, reprinted an extract dealing with the Pillar from *Sketches of Old Dublin*, a book published in 1907, the editor added his own note on the siting of the Pillar, concluding that it was 'high time that the blunder (of putting the Pillar where it was) should be rectified and the Pillar removed to a more suitable site.'[34]

Soon the argument was political and personal. When Dublin Corporation voted in favour of removing the Pillar in 1931 it declared it 'a shame that the English hero, and adulterer, held pride of place in the capital city while there was still no statue to Tone, or Brian Boru or Patrick Sarsfield.'

But the problem remained that no one had the power to remove the Pillar, and no one was offering to pay the cost. In the post-war period, after the Free State became the Republic, the argument became more heated.

O'Connell Street in the 1950s

In 1955 the Corporation formally requested the permission of the Trustees to remove the statue of Nelson from the Pillar and put it in the National Museum. (It wanted Wolfe Tone to replace Nelson on the Pillar.) The Trustees said they could not do that—the terms of the trusteeship imposed on them the duty to 'embellish and uphold the monument in perpetuation of the object for which it was subscribed and erected by the citizens of Dublin'—the honouring of

Nelson. In 1956 Dublin City Council responded that it was intolerable that such a public monument should remain in private hands, and demanded that there should be legislation to enable the Council to '…take possession of the Nelson Pillar with power to remove or demolish the said Pillar in part or in whole as they see fit'.

The Pillar and its fate were also debated briefly at the Northern Ireland Parliament at Stormont in Belfast. In November 1955, Morris May (Ards) asked the Prime Minister, Lord Brookeborough, if he was aware of the desire of the citizens of the Republic that the monument known as Nelson's Pillar should be demolished, and was he prepared to offer to take the monument and have it re-erected in some suitable public place in the city of Belfast.

He got a rather odd reply; Brian Maginness, answering for the PM, said the name of Viscount Nelson occupied a unique position in British history, as a supreme naval strategist. But, displaying a somewhat limited vision of unionism, he went on:

> *Curiously enough, he is also one of the few great British leaders whose origins were not in the North of Ireland. Whilst the Government appreciates the laudable sentiments which inspired the question, the Hon Member should understand that there are many great British leaders whose connections with Northern Ireland are much more close than Lord Nelson's and whom particularly Ulster might well desire to honour by the erection of a suitable tribute to their greatness.*

Mr. May remarked that if space could not be found for Nelson in Belfast he could assure the Minister space could be found for him in the town of Newtownards. Mr. Stewart (East Tyrone) suggested that if the statue did come north, the Minister should ensure that it was ground down and used for road metal for the counties of Tyrone and Fermanagh.[35] (A year earlier, in 1954, Dublin Corporation received an approach, perhaps not entirely serious, from a body calling itself The Port St. Anne Society in Killough in County Down, offering to negotiate for the purchase of the statue of

Nelson, not the Pillar, to be used in their planned restoration of the port of Killough.)

The idea of removing Nelson but retaining the Pillar was gaining support in Dublin, but the inter-party Government of John. A Costello (1954-7) did not share Fianna Fail's zeal. Costello himself said that on historical and artistic grounds the Pillar should be left alone. Desmond Ryan, sometime secretary to Patrick Pearse, argued that Nelson had acquired squatter's rights to his place in O'Connell Street, and praised his unique contribution to the symmetry of the street.

Ryan also raised what he called the almost insoluble problem of finding any suitable tenant for the Pillar, if Nelson was removed. At one time or another, the nominees had included, as well as Tone, Jesus Christ, St Patrick, the Virgin Mary, St Laurence O'Toole, Patrick Pearse, and John F Kennedy.

One of the most resounding defences of the Pillar came in 1955 from Thomas Bodkin, a highly respected figure in Dublin, noted author on art and a former Director of the National Gallery of Ireland. In a talk broadcast on Radio Eireann he described the Pillar with Nelson on it as 'one of the finest statues of its sort in existence...a fluted Doric column of exquisite proportions...the focal point of our lovely city'.

Including it with other monumental pillars in Venice, Paris, Berlin, Rome and London, all distinguishing marks of great capital cities, he declared 'We have the best of the lot. It is all our own work'. In a sadly prophetic comment he added:

> *It is now proposed by some people that it be taken down. Some would like to blow it up and see it crash in fragments in the middle of O'Connell Street.*[36]

Ironically, the problems caused by the Pillar to the traffic in O'Connell Street seemed to have disappeared by the middle of the 20th century. The question of cost, however, remained, and probably helped deter Fianna Fail when it returned to office in 1957, and when the question was raised at Cabinet level in 1959. Even when a specific proposal was made in Cabinet in 1964 to replace the Pillar with a statue of Pearse to mark the 50ᵗʰ anniversary of 1916, the normally decisive Sean Lemass did no more than agree to look at the question.

William III, College Green, departed 1929. W.H.Bartlett c1830.

In fact Nelson and his Pillar had probably been in much greater danger for many years from illegal bombers than from Corporation or Government. King William III's statue in College Green had been blown up in 1929, George II, of St Stephen's Green, went the same way in 1937, Field Marshall Lord Gough in 1957 and Lord Carlisle in 1958. Lord Eglinton, another Viceroy, disappeared from Stephen's Green.

Queen Victoria had suffered the indignity of being hoisted from her seat outside Leinster House in 1948, but at least that was done legally, and there were arguments for it—the statue was generally regarded as ugly and ill-sited; it was right in front of the national legislature, and Ireland had just become a Republic and left the British Commonwealth. Wellington's towering obelisk in the Phoenix Park proved massive enough to defy the dynamiters.

Nelson, on the other hand was extremely vulnerable. He was right in the middle of the city, and very accessible—everyone who paid his admission fee could climb the inner staircase. As events sadly proved, it was not too difficult to blow it up.

Edwardian Dublin (postcard)

A TERRIBLE FATE OF A STAIRS!

Dublin Opinion's comment on the sudden departure of Nelson; March 1966.
Cartoon by Charles E Kelly, © Mr Frank Kelly

On the evening of Monday March 7th 1966, as Dubliners were preparing to mark the golden jubilee of the 1916 Easter Rising, the bombers found their way into Pillar's stairway, and placed their explosives about half way up. At 1.32am on Tuesday March 8th the bomb went off and the upper part of the Pillar crashed into

O'Connell Street. The statue was shattered, the head lying among the rubble.

Reactions to Nelson's sudden departure were varied. There was, as always, the sneaking regard for a bit of bravado and for any violent action in the name of Irish freedom. Indignation at what was called an act of monumental vandalism was partly defused by the prompt composing and recording of a witty ditty entitled '*Up went Nelson and the Pillar too*', which gained immediate popularity. Then thoughts quickly turned to the two-week celebration of the Easter Rising.

The official response to the dynamiting of the Pillar came in a short statement issued by the Government Information Bureau in the name of the Minister for Justice, Mr Brian Lenihan. In it the Minister 'condemned the reckless action of those responsible for the blowing-up of Nelson's Pillar'. He pointed out that the explosion was timed for 1.30 am, when many late-night workers would be in the area, and was without any regard for the lives of citizens. As it was, there was wanton damage to property, and the disruption of traffic had inconvenienced thousands of Dubliners.[37]

In an editorial *The Irish Times* deemed the Minister's statement a 'tepid' reply to what it described as a 'coup in the heart of the capital city' and a direct blow to the prestige of the state and the authority of the Government.

There was almost certainly anger in government circles at what was clearly an attempt by subversives to hi-jack the official celebrations of the 50th anniversary, particularly in the context of the then Taoiseach Sean Lemass's recent peaceful overtures to the new Northern Ireland Prime Minister, Terence O'Neill.

But there was an equally obvious desire to play down the significance of the explosion, hence Mr Lenihan's dismissal of it as a 'reckless action' which had disrupted traffic and inconvenienced Dubliners. (Almost half a century later one historian has described the demolition of the Pillar as the 'iconic moment' of the jubilee celebration, and a 'most dramatic reconfiguring of the nation's capital'.[38])

No one was ever charged with, let alone convicted of the blowing up of the Pillar, though it was assumed at the time that it was the work of the outlawed Irish Republican Army, or of people associated with it.[39] (The Republican Movement disclaimed responsibility at the time.[40]) Generally, there was regret that the city's most prominent landmark had gone, and that the principal street of the capital was not what it was. Looking back on its destruction Owen Sheehy-Skeffington told the Senate that he had felt a sense of loss, not because of Nelson but because the Pillar symbolised for many Dubliners the centre of the city. 'It had a certain rugged, elegant, grace about it...'

The 1969 Nelson Pillar Act terminated the Nelson Pillar Trust, and vested in Dublin Corporation the site where the Pillar had stood. It awarded the Trustees £21,170 in compensation for the destruction of the Pillar, and additional compensation for loss of earnings from admission fees.

The almost invisible base of the Spire

That was not quite the end of the story. In 1987 the Metropolitan Streets Commission proposed that the Pillar be rebuilt, but found no takers. The following year architects, artists and sculptors came together to mount the Pillar Project, and invited proposals for what might be done to replace the Pillar. This resulted in 17 imaginative submissions, some very strange indeed. The Pillar Project was a theoretical frolic for artistic imaginations, related to the celebration of the City's own millennium and not a competition for real proposals.

The Spire towers over the GPO

That came later, in 1997, when the Dublin Corporation decided to replace the Pillar and hold an international competition for a design for a new monument on the site to mark the year 2000 and the start of the new millennium.

The winner was Ian Ritchie's *Spire of Dublin*, named the Millennium Spire, which now graces O'Connell Street. 120 metres high it is three times as tall as Nelson's Pillar, but extremely slender, even at its street-level base. Giles Worsley, the *Daily Telegraph's* architectural guru, described it as:

> *...a feat of astonishing technical competence, a truly 21ˢᵗ century monument which does not proclaim the authority of a king or a conqueror, nor memorialise some terrible act of savagery. Instead it is an affirmation of the essential optimism of the human spirit. The Spire captures the spirit of the new Ireland, healing the wounds of earlier nationalisms while promising the revival of what should be a great European boulevard.*[41]

Dublin's Fallen Hero

It is hard to find any such enthusiasm for The Spike, as the Spire is commonly known, among Dubliners, though some are beginning to warm to it a little, especially since the improvements to the centre of O'Connell Street. Viewed from O'Connell Bridge, or from down Henry Street or Talbot Street it is very striking indeed, quite beautiful. At its base the contrast with the Pillar could not be more remarkable—the Spike at street level is unobtrusive to the point almost of invisibility.

But, Dubliners ask, what does it stand for? The Spike means nothing— it is beautiful and well designed, but it has nothing to do with Dublin or Ireland. And you can't climb it—there is no public access.

It is not, it has been argued, a monument at all, for the Millennium was a global concept and an artificial one. The Pillar, on the other hand, was all about this island's history—about great events of which Trafalgar was one, about the relationship of Ireland with England, and about the golden period of Georgian architecture in Dublin. Destruction of the Pillar robbed O'Connell Street of both drama and history.

A half century has erased almost all trace of the massive Pillar which once dominated the city centre. One reminder is still to be seen in nearby Talbot Street, where the sign for the Pillar Bed and Breakfast establishment (above) now shares the view with the Spire.

7   A LOFTY ARCH

Castletownshend, Co Cork.
The Nelson Arch stood on a high point along the ridge to the right.

The Dublin Pillar was not the only, or indeed the first monument erected to Nelson in Ireland. On November 10th, 1805—only two days after news of Trafalgar reached Dublin, and a full week before the inaugural meeting of the 'bankers, merchants and citizens' of Dublin to discuss their proposed monument—a substantial, if rough, stone arch was erected on a hilltop near Castletownshend in west Cork in memory of Nelson.

Like the Pillar it survived as a prominent local landmark for more than a century and a half, before it too fell victim to politically motivated vandalism, finally being totally destroyed in 1976.

This Nelson Arch, as it was known, was the work of Captain Joshua Rowley Watson R.N., then commander of the Sea Fencibles based in Castletownshend. A marble tablet affixed to the arch stated:

Dublin's Fallen Hero

This arch, the first monument erected to the memory of Nelson after the battle of Trafalgar, was sketched and planned by Captain Joshua Rowley Watson R.N., and built by him and twelve hundred of the Sea Fencibles then under his command (assisted by eight masons). It was erected in five hours on the 10th of November.

The Sea Fencibles were an auxiliary naval force recruited from seamen and fishermen as part of the augmented defence against a possible French invasion following the resumption of the war with Napoleonic France in 1803. They were divided into twenty districts around the Irish coast, mainly the western and southern seaboard, with serving Royal Naval officers in command of each district. Captain Watson was in charge of the County Cork coast from Mizen Head to Galley Head, with his headquarters in Castletownshend. An official report of 1804 shows that he had 203 boats and 898 men under his command there, so his claim that he had twelve hundred helpers when he built the arch the following year may not be so outrageous as it sounds.

The arch stood on the highest point, known as Mount Eagle, of the line of hills overlooking the long inlet of Castlehaven, within the estate of the Townshend family, the builders of Castletownshend. The family in residence in 1805 would have had a particular interest in Nelson's great victory. The second son, John, barely 16 years old, had joined the army as a cornet in January 1805, and was later to serve under Wellington in the Peninsular War in the early stages of a 40 year career with the Light Dragoons. The head of the household in 1805 was Richard Boyle Townshend, who had served as a Member of the Irish Parliament and had been among those who opposed its abolition.

Several 19th century travellers were mightily impressed by the arch. Lady Georgina Chatterton, in her *Rambles in the South of Ireland in the Year 1838*, records seeing on the summit of one of the rocky headlands that surround Castletownshend '.. a lofty arch erected in the memory of Nelson by a party of officers.'

A Lofty Arch

It is formed of large stones, without cement, and I was told it was constructed after church one Sunday...This wonderful arch forms a fine object in most of the views about Castletownshend, and as I first saw it towering above the mist which concealed the base of the mountain height on which it stood, its appearance was supernatural.

Lady Chatterton was not entirely convinced that the monument had been constructed in one afternoon, noting that the story reminded her of the 'tale related in Ireland of every colossal structure, that it was the work of one night.'[42]

That Capt. Watson's arch was the first monument erected to Nelson anywhere in the world can hardly be doubted. It is not clear how news of Trafalgar and Nelson's death arrived so quickly in West Cork, only two days after it reached Dublin. One local tradition has it that a ship on its way home from Trafalgar, or from the vicinity of the battle, put into Castlehaven and that its crew came ashore and built the arch. Naval records show no evidence of this, but it is possible that Captain Watson may have had early news of Nelson's death from a passing ship. Stephen Gwynn, in his 1927 book *Ireland*, recommends to visitors 'the rough stone arch set up overlooking the harbour, in memory of the day when a swift frigate bringing up from the south put in here and brought to these islands the first news of Trafalgar."[43]

The arch is mentioned in *The Nelson Memorial*, by John Knox Laughton, (1896), as 'first in point of time' among the many hundreds of monuments to Nelson. He records the inscription on the marble tablet, adding that the tablet had been broken off many years previously and had long since disappeared. Of the arch itself he says it was hastily built of dry stones and 'is now no better than a ruin'.[44]

However, one of the few images that have survived of the arch dates from that same year, 1896. It is a photograph reproduced in the Journal of the Cork Historical and Archaeological Society taken by a Mr Coghill on the 21st October, 1896, the anniversary of Trafalgar. It shows the arch largely intact, but with vegetation sprouting from it. [45]

The first mention of politically motivated damage to the arch comes in 1920, when according to some accounts it was 'destroyed' during the War of Independence, and re-erected two years later.[46] More likely the arch was vandalised at that time rather than destroyed, and was presumably repaired by the Townshend family of Castletownshend, on whose land it stood. It was again attacked in 1966, the fiftieth anniversary of the 1916 Rising, this time so seriously that the Townshend family could do little more than erect a much smaller version from the wreckage.[47]

The Nelson Arch as it was in 1896.
(Courtesy of the Cork Historical & Archaeological Society)

That in its turn was demolished in 1976. Soon intensive forestry on the hilltop had begun to obscure any view of the remains of the arch, and today all trace of it has disappeared.

Captain Watson, however, lives on in his paintings and sketches. He was a gifted water-colourist, and in 1816 and 1817, after the end of the Napoleonic wars, he took leave of absence from the Royal Navy to tour the eastern United States, filling two notebooks with views of Washington, Philadelphia, Boston, the Hudson valley in New York and other places.[48]

The tablet originally attached to the arch at Castletownshend tells us that it was built according to sketches made by Captain Watson, and it is unthinkable that such an avid artist did not record the finished arch in a sketchbook. We know he returned to Ireland in 1815 and did a drawing entitled *Wood Scenery on the grounds of Castletownshend*, but no drawing of the arch has come to light.[49] Though born in England, Watson had Irish origins. His grandfather had been the Church of Ireland Rector at Ennis, in County Clare, and a sister of Watson was still living there in 1815.

©*Dublin City Council.*
(Photo Alastair Seaton.)

In addition to the severed head of Nelson, recovered, eventually, from the wreckage of the Pillar, and now permanently on display in the Reading Room of the Dublin City Archive in Pearse Street in Dublin, (right) there is one surviving memorial in Ireland to Nelson.

In Dervock, in north Antrim, in a hall belonging to St Coleman's Church of Ireland, a striking stained glass triptych depicts the moment on the poop deck of the *Victory* when Nelson ordered the flying of the 'England Expects' signal just before the Battle of Trafalgar.[50] The central panel shows Nelson in conversation with Captain Blackwood from County Down, (with hat in hand). The panel to the right shows Captain William Adair, from County Antrim, (the right of two men in red jackets) the commander of the marine force on the *Victory*, who was to die alongside Nelson.

The hall was built in 1936 by the Allen family of Dervock, who had been linked by marriage in the 19th century to Captain Adair's family. Its purpose was to honour, not just Nelson and Adair, but also, in another triptych, two later forebears of the Allens—General Sir William Adair, of the Royal Marines, and Rear Admiral Thomas Benjamin Stratton Adair. A smaller window shows the *Victory* locked in conflict with the French ship *Redoubtable*.

The Trafalgar memorial window in Dervock, County Antrim.

Walker of Derry, another victim of monumental vandalism: departed 1973.
19th century print from drawing by T.M.Baynes, c 1830.

The mania for monumental and architectural destruction that seized elements of Irish nationalism in the late 19th and 20th centuries has left the country immeasurably poorer. As Owen Sheehy Skeffington told the Senate in the aftermath of the dynamiting of Nelson's Pillar, 'The man who destroyed the Pillar made Dublin look more like Birmingham and less like an ancient city on the River Liffey — the Pillar gave Dublin an internationally known appearance.' Ireland's foremost poet, William Butler Yeats, who did not think much of the architectural merits of the Pillar, and would have been happy to see it moved, nevertheless wanted it preserved. In 1923 he declared that...

It represents the feeling of Protestant Ireland for a man who helped break the power of Napoleon. The life and work of the people who erected it is a part of our tradition. I think we should accept the whole past of this nation, and not pick and choose.[51]

In a biting short poem entitled *The Three Monuments,* written in the 1920s, Yeats refers to where…

> *… our most renowned patriots stand,*
> *One among the birds of the air;*
> *A stumpier on either hand:*

The point of the poem is to poke fun at Ireland's post-independence political leaders who had made O'Connell Street their favourite site for rallies where they could lecture the populous on the purity of Irishness while, up above, in Yeats' words:

> *The three old rascals laugh out loud.*

The old rascals are, of course, O'Connell, Nelson and Parnell, and the poet claims all three as *our* most renowned patriots, reaffirming his belief that Nelson and the elite of Dublin who had erected the Pillar represent one tradition in Ireland's past, and one strand of what constitutes Irishness.

James Joyce, from a different tradition, said something similar. In response to a comment from a friend in 1919 on the fighting in Ireland and relations between England and Ireland, he replied:

> *Ireland is what she is, and therefore I am what I am, because of relations that have existed between England and Ireland. Tell me why you think I ought to change the conditions that gave Ireland and me a shape and a destiny?*[52]

Yeats and Joyce were both speaking at a time when the newly independent Irish state was busily redefining Irishness in the opposite direction and the narrowest possible manner by eliminating or seeking to downgrade all that was British or English, including the language. That Nelson and his Pillar survived is perhaps evidence that not many people subscribed fully to such an ideology and while they may not have articulated their position as clearly as those two writers, they shared an awareness of the diversity of traditions in the island, and saw the Pillar as part of what they were.

Even while the Irish Free State's post-independence administration was busily setting about the task of de-anglicising Irish life and culture, the man at its head, John A Costello, the man who later made Ireland a republic, was ready to defend the Pillar on 'historical and artistic grounds'.

Others prominent in the new dispensation, like Thomas Bodkin and Desmond Ryan, found grounds to resist calls for the Pillar's removal. Ryan's wry comment that Nelson's century and a half in residence had given him 'squatters rights' was a humorous way of saying that the Pillar and its occupant had become so much part of Dublin that there was no reason to remove either of them.

Another writer, Oliver St John Gogarty, declared the Pillar 'the greatest thing we have in Dublin'. In *As I was going down Sackville Street* (1935) he recounts his reaction to a glimpse of the Pillar:

> *I gazed up Sackville Street. The grandest thing we have in Dublin, the great Doric column that upheld the Admiral was darkened by flying mists, intermittent as battle smoke; but aloft in light silvery as the moonshine of legend, the statue in whiter stone gazed forever southwards towards Trafalgar and the Nile. That Pillar marks the end of a civilization, the culmination of the great period of eighteenth-century Dublin…The men who first founded this city set up their Pillar…. How long, I thought, would it be before the Gael if left to himself would have set a Pillar up? A long time…*
>
> *We are not Pillar builders, nor do we erect trophies, and we shall never erect anything so long as we keep up the pose of setting our faces against Empire and Conquerors and soldiers of trophies…Yet all we have, and most of what we are, proceed from these strong sources.*[53]

After the accession to power in 1933 of De Valera and the Fianna Fail party, the more republican element of the original Sinn Fein movement, the administration still managed to ignore or side-line repeated calls for the removal of Nelson.

In 1960, as the clamour mounted with the approach of the 50th anniversary of the Easter Rising, one leading figure in the Dublin

Dublin's Fallen Hero

art world, Beatrice Glenavy R.H.A. in a letter to the *Irish Times* denounced such calls as evidence of 'the destructive genius of the Irish people'. To the objection to Nelson because he was an Englishman, she responded that it was surely time '..we became less parochial and provincial. Could we not look on that great one-eyed and one-armed sailor as a symbol of human heroism?'

Lady Glenavy ended her letter with an appeal:- 'in the name of all that has elegance, splendour, beauty and dignity, leave the Pillar alone'.[54] It was not to be; six years later the Pillar was destroyed. Within a few years the IRA had added the Caledon column in County Tyrone and the Walker Memorial on Derry's walls to its trophies.

The Earl of Caledon, when, in 1807, he gave his generous £100 to help finance the column to honour Nelson, was not to know that he too, like Nelson, would end up on top of a Doric column, sculpted by the same Thomas Kirk. The column was erected, two years after his death, by his grateful tenantry on his own estate at Caledon in County Tyrone in 1841. A century and a half later, he too, would, like Nelson, be blown off his column by the zealots of the IRA.

Derry, like Dublin, is a poorer place without its column. The Memorial column on which the Rev George Walker stood until 1973 was similar to Nelson's Pillar. (It too had a staircase inside.) While there were those who thought the Rev Walker's role as co-Governor of the city in the defence of Derry during the siege of 1688-89 was not as heroic as he himself had suggested, his column was superbly situated on the walls and was a striking monument to the siege and all the defenders.

For years both Walker and his column were divisive icons in a divided city. Today, the siege, and the walls which remain from it, are among Derry's chief claims to eminence. But we can no longer go and climb Walker's winding stair to look down across the walled city and the River Foyle.

While the loss of irreplaceable historic monuments is regrettable, they were minor casualties in an orgy of terrorism and counter-terrorism which cost more than 3500 lives over 30 years. But their destruction was also indicative of a dogmatic mind set which saw no space in Ireland for strands and traditions outside its own fanatical nationalism, and sought to change history by destroying the physical evidence of such strands.

The ten years from 2012 on have been dubbed the Decade of Centenaries, beginning with the Ulster Covenant in 1912, through the Easter Rising and the Somme in 1916, to, from 1919 to 1922, the War of Independence, partition, and the establishment of Northern Ireland and the Irish Free State.

The fact that these commemorations are equally divided between the broadly nationalist and unionist traditions on the island has prompted some soul-searching on their shared history, and on relations between Ireland and Britain, a rethinking already underway since the negotiation of the Belfast Agreement in the 1990s. A landmark in this evolution was, in 2011, the first visit by a reigning British monarch to southern Ireland since partition.

In the middle of the decade comes the 50th anniversary of the destruction of Nelson's Pillar, so perhaps we should revisit the Pillar in the light of this rethinking. A passage in the Belfast Agreement, of which Sinn Fein was one of the chief architects, commits future governments of Ireland, south and north, to govern with...

....rigorous impartiality on behalf of all the people in diversity of their identities and traditions...and of parity of esteem, and of just and equal treatment for the identity, ethos and aspirations of both communities.

That formula would seem to guarantee Nelson and his statue at least equal standing – give or take about 100 feet—with his neighbours O'Connell and Parnell.

When Desmond Ryan praised 'Nelson's unique contribution to the symmetry' of O'Connell Street, he was thinking in architectural terms of the streetscape and the monument. In retrospect Nelson was also adding some symmetry in political terms to a real understanding of Ireland and Irishness, positioned as he was between O'Connell and Parnell, and alongside the GPO. If still there he would be a visual reminder, not just of a golden age of architecture in Dublin but of the convoluted relationship between Britain and Ireland which, as Joyce said, has made Ireland what it now is.

Amongst Dublin's greatest claims to distinction today, and the main reasons people want to visit it, are its Georgian architecture and its literary heritage. Nelson's Pillar was the most conspicuous if not the most elegant example of Georgian building, and by far the easiest and cheapest to visit and explore. It also provided, after the publication of *Ulysses,* a unique link with Joyce and his Dublin.

Its destruction has robbed generations of Irish people of an object lesson in their own history, and of the chance of rubbing shoulders with visiting crowds of Nelson and Joyce enthusiasts scrambling up the rough stone spiral staircase to the platform just below the Admiral.

Dublin is indeed a poorer place without the Pillar.

The Second Earl of Caledon on his pillar in County Tyrone . Blown up in 1973.

Leabharlanna Poibli Chathair Bhaile Átha Cliath
Dublin City Public Libraries

NOTES

[1] *Freeman's Journal*, 9/02/1805.

[2] Details of this and other meetings relating to the building of the Pillar are found in *Nelson's Pillar; A Description of the Pillar with a list of subscribers, etc.*published by order of the committee, reprinted in 1846.
by Patrick Henchy in Dublin Historical Record, Vol 10, 1948.

[3] *Freeman's Journal* 10/2/1805.

[4] See Conservation Report on the Birr Monument by Howley, Hayes Architects, February 2009.

[5] *History of the City of Dublin*, by J.T.Gilbert, first published in 1861. Vol 3, p20, 1974 reprint, Royal Irish Academy.

[6] See *Sunday Press*, 4 March 1956. Article by Gerard Maguire.

[7] *The Irish Builder*, 20 June, 1923

[8] See *Drawings from the Irish Architectural Archive* by D J Griffin and S Lincoln. Dublin 1993. p 51.

[9] *Nelson's Pillar; A Description of the Pillar*, published by the committee in 1811 and reprinted in 1846.

[10] Liscombe, R.W., *William Wilkins 1778-1839*, Cambridge University Press, 1980, p 58.

[11] Maurice Craig *Dublin 1660-1860*, Dublin 1980, p 287.

[12] Edward McParland, in his comprehensive survey of Johnston's life and work concludes that the vast scale of the Pillar makes it unlike anything Johnston could have designed. (*Quarterly Bulletin of the Irish Georgian Society*, Vol XII, no 3,4. 1969.

[13] See the Great Yarmouth monument web site nelsonsmonument.org.uk. The county of Norfolk had, like Dublin, launched an immediate appeal in November 1805 to raise money for a monument to Nelson. The project was abandoned due to the poor response, but another appeal was made by Great Yarmouth in 1814. The initial estimate of the cost of erecting Wilkins' proposed column is given as £7,500 – almost exactly the same as the final cost of the Dublin Pillar.

[14] Peter, A *Sketches of Old Dublin*, Dublin, 1907.

[15]. Quoted in *The Irish Builder*, July 15, 1882, p208. A detailed description of the procession and the ceremony appeared in the *Evening Correspondent* of 16 February, 1808, and is included in *And Nelson on his Pillar*, by Bolger and Share. Dublin 1976.

[16] *Nelson's Pillar; A Description of the Pillar*, op cit..

[17] House of Commons Debates, 28 January, 1806. Vol6 cc 97-107.

[18] *Nelson's Pillar; A Description of the Pillar, op cit.*

[19] The September 1809 issue of the *Irish Magazine* records that the statue had been placed on the column.

[20] Mary Moutray was the wife of Captain Moutray, Dockyard Commissioner at Antigua when Nelson, aged 25, served there in 1784. After her husband's death she retired to Ireland. News of Nelson's death was sent to by Collingwood – who

had also fallen for her charms in the West Indies. Her husband belonged to the Moutray family of Favor Royal, near Augher in County Tyrone.

[21] Pocock, Tom, *Horatio Nelson* Pimlico, London 1994. p 72.

[22] Tim Clayton & Phil Craig: *Trafalgar, the men, the battle and the storm*, BCA, 2004. p 42. Irish recruitment to the Royal Navy was almost certainly boosted by the distressed conditions in Ireland after 1798 and by heightened impressment of merchant seamen on the resumption of war in 1803.

[23] *Nelson's Surgeon* by L W B Brockliss, John Cardwell and Michael Moss. OUP. 2005.

[24] *Robert Emmet, A Life* by Patrick Geoghegan. Dublin, 2004. p 101.

[25] *Correspondence of Daniel O'Connell*; by Maurice O'Connell. vol I, 97. IUP, Dublin.,

[26] Andrew Lambert, *Nelson, Britannia's God of War,* Faber, London, 2004. pp. xv and xviii.

[27] MacDonagh, Oliver. *O'Connell,* Weidenfeld and Nicolson, London 1991. p102.

[28], Maurice Craig, *Dublin 1660—1860*, Dublin 1952. P 287. (1980 edit.)

[29] *The Irish Builder,* op cit. (At that time the Irish Builder estimated the cost of relocating the Pillar at £4,000. Eight years earlier 'An Architect' writing to the magazine in support of moving the Pillar had estimated the cost at £1,500 and suggested this could be raised by public subscription. *The Irish Builder*, 15 Feb., 1874, p 149.)

[30] *The Irish Builder* 15 July, 1890 p 175.

[31] Penguin Classics edition of *Ulysses,* (200). p.147.

[32] *Ibid* p 615.

[33] See *The Easter Rising* by Michael Foy and Brian Barton. Sutton Publishing. Shroud. 1999. p 175.

[34] *The Irish Builder and Engineer,* June 30, 1923, p 497.

[35] NI Parliament, House of Commons Debates vol XXXIX, cols 2896, 2897. 9th Nov 1955.

[36] National Archives TAOIS/S4523 C/61.

[37] *Irish Times,* March 9, 1966. P 1.

[38] See "Where Nelson's Pillar was Not" in *Transforming 1916, Meaning, Memory and the Fiftieth Anniversary of the Easter Rising,* by Roisin Higgins. Cork University Press, 2012.

[39] The consensus now is that the culprits were a small number of dissidents led by Joe Christle who had split from the IRA,. See Richard English's *Armed Struggle: A History of the IRA*, Macmillan, 2003. p72.

[40] *Irish Times,* March 9, 1966.

[41] *Daily Telegraph*, 16th August, 2003.

[42] *Rambles in the South of Ireland in the Year 1838* by Lady Georgina Chatterton.

[43] *Ireland; Its places of beauty entertainment sport and historic association*, by Stephen Gwynn. Harrap, 1927. p 169.

[44] *The Nelson Memorial,* by John Knox Laughton, London 1896, p 320.

[45] *Journal of Cork Historical and Archaeological Society*, Series 2,vol III pp. 228-229 1897.

[46] *Southern Star*, 2nd April, 1966.

[47] This attack on the arch came after the explosion at Nelson's Pillar, and may have been in response to an item in the Skibbereen *Southern Star* of April 2nd, 1966, showing a picture of the arch under a headline NELSON ARCH STILL STANDS.

[48] Two sketch books survive, one is held by the New-York Historical Society, the other by the Barra Foundation, in Wayne, Pennsylvania.

[49] An account of Captain Watson's life was published in 1997 by the Barra Foundation and the University of Pennsylvania Press. The author, Professor Kathleen A Foster, mentions the *Wood Scenery* drawing and locates it in the 'Pope collection', drawings held, in 1997, by Capt. Watson's descendant Elizabeth Burgess Pope. Unfortunately it has not been possible to trace this collection. (*Captain Watson's Travels in America: the Sketchbooks and Diary of Joshua Rowley Watson 1771-1818*, by Kathleen A Foster, University of Pennsylvania Press, 1997)

[50] The window was designed and installed by the London firm of Heaton, Butler and Boyne.

[51] Statement to the press, quoted in "Nelson's Pillar" by Patrick Henchy in Dublin Historical Record, vol x, 1948, p 63.

[52] Conversation recorded by Frank Budgen in his *James Joyce and the Making of Ulysses*, p 155. OUP, 1972.

[53] *As I was Going Down Sackville Street*, Sphere Books 1968 edition, 1980 reprint pp. 263-4.

[54] *Irish Times*, January 11, 1960.

Select Bibliography

No book dealing specifically with Nelson's Pillar has appeared since William Bolger and Bernard Share's *And Nelson on his Pillar, A Retrospective Record* (Nonpareil, Dublin 1976),a mainly light-hearted but informative anthology of writing about the Pillar from 1808 to 1966. Up to now the standard published account of the Pillar has been Patrick Henchy's 'Nelson's Pillar', which appeared in the Dublin Historical Record, Vol 10, 1948.

Nelson's Pillar, A Description of the Pillar, with A List of Subscribers is an invaluable first-hand account of the origins of the Pillar compiled by the Nelson Pillar Committee in 1811, and reissued in 1846. The growing interest in the history of Irish architecture and public sculpture in recent decades has seen frequent reference to the Pillar in books and journal articles; a selection is listed here:

Books

Brady, Joseph and Simms, Annegret, *Dublin through Space and Time,* Four Courts Press, 2001.

Craig, Maurice, *Dublin 1660-1860,* Allen Figgis, 1952.

Hill, Judith, *Irish Public Sculpture: A History,* Four Courts Press, 1998.

Higgins, Roisin, *Transforming 1916 : meaning, memory and the fiftieth anniversary of the Easter Rising,* Cork University Press, 2012.

Liscombe, R.W., *William Wilkins 1778-1839,* Cambridge University Press, 1980

Murphy, Paula, *Nineteenth Century Irish Sculpture,* Yale University Press, 2010

O'Regan, John, *A Monument in the City: Nelson's Pillar and its aftermath,* Kinsale – Gandon Editions, 1998.

Articles:

Edward. McParland, 'Francis Johnston, Architect', *Bulletin of the Irish Georgian Society* Vol XII, 3&4, 1969.

Paula Murphy,' The Politics of the Street Monument', *Irish Arts Review,* 1994.

Micheal O Riain, 'Nelson's Pillar: a controversy that ran and ran', *History Ireland,* vol 6, No 4, winter 1998.

Andrew Thacker, 'Toppling Masonry and Textual Space; Nelson's Pillar and the Spatial Politics of Ulysses', *Irish Studies Review,* 8.2. 2010.

Yvonne Whelan, 'Monuments, power and contested space – the iconography of Sackville Street before independence' *Irish Geography,* vol 34:1.

Yvonne Whelan, 'Symbolising the State; the iconography of O'Connell Street' *Irish Geography,* vol 34.2.

ALSO BY DENNIS KENNEDY

Yankee Doodles. Ormeau Books. 2012.
"...vignettes, some amusing, some amazing, offering a short time capsule of America before Vietnam." Sean Farrell, *Irish Independent.*

Square Peg. Nonsuch. 2009.
".. an affectionate and somewhat wry account of working at The Irish Times and living in Dublin.....finely observed moments and surprising recollections." Michael Foley, *The Irish Times.*

Climbing Slemish: An Ulster Memoir. Trafford, 2006.
*"An engrossing story, recounted with charm and exuberance..."*Patricia Craig, *The Irish Times.*

The Widening Gulf. Blackstaff, 1988.
"..splendid...sufficiently contentious to warrant extensive concern and glowing reviews." J.Bowyer Bell, *Sunday Tribune.*

Information on publications at; www.denniskennedy.eu

Dennis Kennedy has worked as a journalist in Northern Ireland, the United States, Ethiopia and for *The Irish Times* in Dublin. He served as Head of the European Commission office in Belfast from 1985 to 1991, and has lectured in European Studies at Queen's University Belfast. Born in Lisburn, Co.Antrim, he was educated at Wallace High School, Queen's University, Belfast, and Trinity College Dublin.